How To BUILD Your Network Marketing TRAVEL Business FAST

KEITH & TOM "BIG AL" SCHREITER

Published by Fortune Network Publishing
PO Box 890084
Houston, TX 77289 USA
+1 (281) 280-9800

BigAlBooks.com

Print ISBN: 978-1-956171-29-7
Ebook ISBN: 978-1-956171-30-3
Audiobook ISBN: 978-1-956171-31-0

Important Disclaimer

This book is written for network marketing professionals interested in promoting travel products, travel clubs, travel income opportunities, or travel-related services.

This is a marketing and mindset book, not professional, tax, investment, or legal advice.

Network marketing and travel-related businesses are regulated in most countries. Rules concerning income claims, earnings representations, advertising, recruiting language, data privacy (GDPR, CCPA, etc.), pyramid scheme laws, travel seller of travel registration, consumer protection, cross-border sales, and more differ between jurisdictions.

We are responsible for proper licenses, registrations, and following applicable laws and regulations in every country, state, or region where we market or enroll customers.

Please follow your company's Policies and Procedures, Income Disclosure Statement, and approved marketing materials guidelines.

Use this material responsibly, ethically, and legally.

CONTENTS

PREFACE

"The world is a book, and if you don't travel, you've only seen one page"

—Unknown

Travel is fun. It's a dream for many.

If we can provide people with better travel options, they will love it. The keyword here is "options."

When we have something most people want, we don't have to sell, manipulate, persuade, or convince. We simply offer our option and allow people to make the choice that works for them.

So relax. Enjoy the experience. Share what we have.

Our mission is only to share this option with others. We will honor their choices.

Get 2 FREE Big Al Training Audios
Magic Words for Prospecting

Plus a Free eBook and the Big Al Newsletter!

BigAlBooks.com/free

Big Al Workshops and Live Online Trainings

BigAlBooks.com/workshops

HERE IS THE SHORT STORY

Not everyone likes chocolate.

Not everyone likes Mercedes cars.

Not everyone likes the latest hit movie.

And yet, all of these things still do a pretty good business.

So, let's talk about travel.

Imagine this: half the people we talk to hate to travel, hate vacations, can't afford a day off work, or even insist on spending their holidays in their mother-in-law's apartment surrounded by 32 cats.

And you know what?

That's okay.

But, the other half?

They dream of luxury vacations. They see a trip as a big, well-earned reward after a year of hard work. Or they just want to travel within a reasonable budget. And if they can save some money on those adventures, even better.

We help these people. We give them more options they didn't know about.

Our job isn't to convert the cat-lovers into beach-goers. We're not here to twist anyone's arm. Instead, we show travel-lovers that they can turn that dream vacation into a reality a little more often, a little more affordably, and with a lot less hassle.

Our mission is not to change people's minds or to sell them something they don't want.

Our mission is to offer help to those who want it.

End of story.

WHO DO I TALK TO?

Someone always asks:

"My brother-in-law would never want to travel. How do I convince him?"

Short answer?

We don't.

Our brother-in-law already knows what's best for his life right now. Relax. He's simply part of the half of the population that is not our market.

And that's okay.

- Not everyone likes chocolate
- Not everyone likes luxury cars
- Not everyone wants to leave their house
- Not everyone wants to travel and see the world

Trying to "convince" people who don't want what we offer is exhausting, awkward, and completely unnecessary.

The big relief

We are not responsible for changing people's minds. And, we are not responsible for:

- Their travel preferences
- Their budget choices

- Their stress level
- Their past experiences
- Their mood five minutes before we spoke to them

They are the experts on their own lives. Let them be.

But should we still mention our business and what we offer?

Yes.

Just not the way most people do. We don't want to sound like a walking brochure or a late-night infomercial.

We offer the option. And then, we stop talking.

- Maybe it's not for them now
- Maybe it will be in six months
- Maybe never

That's their decision.

What we don't do is withhold the option "just in case" they don't like it. That's not respectful. They deserve to have a choice.

Our job is simple

We could say:

"Here's an option you may not know about."

What they do with that option is entirely up to them.

Why this polite approach works

We never know:

- What's happening in someone's finances
- What stress they're under
- What travel experience went wrong last year
- What memories they associate with vacations

People carry invisible baggage. Some of the baggage is good. Some of the baggage might scare them away from our option. We don't know. We are not their baggage handlers.

When we respect their choices, conversations feel lighter.

And the good news is, most people become more curious.

So, how do we bring up this option?

"How do I talk about this socially?"

"How do I not sound salesy?"

"How do I make it feel normal?"

The good news is we don't have to introduce everything at once.

We don't have to say, "Sit down and listen to everything I know about my business."

They will hate that. So instead of pitching, selling, educating, explaining, and boring them to death, what should we do?

Let's introduce a conversation

An example? We could calmly mention:

"I travel a little differently now. I found a way to get better travel options and save a lot of money."

And then … we stop talking. That was easy.

If they're interested, they'll ask us to continue the conversation.

If they're not interested, they won't.

Our job is to open the door, not push them through it. People can feel when we have an agenda.

Remember this. If people feel pressured, they will resist. So no judging or chasing. Simply hold the door open and let them decide to continue the conversation or not.

WHAT TO SAY / WHAT NOT TO SAY

Are we ready to cringe?

Think of how we would feel if someone approached us like this?

"You should really join this travel program!"

Yikes! Sounds like an incoming sales pitch from an over-caffeinated salesman. This opening certainly causes people to back away.

"This membership will change your life!"

Now, that is a big promise. They'll think, "Uh-oh, what's the catch?"

"You're missing out if you don't do this."

More pressure. Someone is trying to make us feel guilty.

"Let me explain how it all works."

Sounds like a huge time-wasting presentation is about to happen … before we even know if we are interested or not.

"Well, I can assure you that our travel prices are the lowest. Plus, we have over 1,000 testimonials already. Our travel resource guru is faster and can beat up every competitor on the internet."

Ugh! Sounds like a salesman with an agenda.

Or worse yet:

"We are a cooperative travel connection company that has high discount contracts with many of the most famous suppliers. We have surety bonds with the IATA and the government licensing department, so you know your deposits are safe with us. Our executive team has 141 years of travel experience. We won an award two years ago. Because of our group buying power, we can provide low prices on your next cruise or vacation. I can send you the link to watch our company video."

Okay, we get the point. These are not good ways to start our conversations. These are not conversation "icebreakers." These are conversation "ice makers."

Conversation openings like these cause people to run away, screaming, "Run! Run! Save yourself!"

What to say instead?

Let's try to create a little curiosity. We could start by saying:

"I found a way to make my travel a lot more affordable."

Most people like saving money. They will want to know more.

"I just found out a neat little travel hack that's been saving me a bundle."

Now we are sharing a cool secret, not delivering an ugly sales pitch.

"I can get some of my trips at wholesale prices now instead of paying retail."

Our prospects will be thinking, "Hey, I would like to do this too!"

"This isn't for everyone, but it sure has been great for me."

Ah, curiosity at its finest. Of course, they want us to continue.

Our prospects can now choose to ask us to continue, or they could change the subject to talking about sports, the weather, or shopping. That would be a hint to us that they are not interested.

And let's remember. Half of the people won't be interested, but we don't know if they will be interested or not … until we talk to them.

More good news?

Even if they are not interested now, we've planted a seed without making it awkward. Who knows what will change in their lives in the future?

HERE IS THE BIG PICTURE

Before we go to more opening sentences, let's step back and look at the big picture. This will explain a lot.

#1: What we offer is better than what they have now

Oh. Let's never forget this.

Want proof? Ask 100 people the following question:

Q. "Would you like to pay less for your travel, or pay more?"

What do you think they would say?

Or ask, "For the same price, would you like a super holiday, or just an ordinary holiday?"

Not too hard to guess their answers.

Or let's ask these 100 people, "Would you like more travel options, or less travel options?"

Uh, we get the idea. What we offer is better.

But what about our business opportunity?

Ask, "Do you want more money in your life, or less money?"

Even the most math-challenged people will answer, "Well, I wasn't good at math in school, but I think I would choose more money."

Or ask, "Would you like to be your own boss, or take orders from someone else?"

Again, most people would prefer freedom.

Okay … but what does this all mean?

We don't need to:

- Sell
- Convince
- Manipulate
- Persuade
- Overexplain
- Pressure
- Twist arms
- Chase

Woah! What???

Yes, people can make a decision if they want something better or not. We don't have to do long presentations, power closing sales techniques, or stalking follow-up calls.

If what we offer is better, it can stand on its own. We don't have to push people uphill. We simply let them know there is an option for a better path forward.

This is like discovering that we can buy the same groceries for half the price without changing stores. Simple and clear.

Do we feel relieved already?

But … we let them choose what is best for them.

If they choose to not take advantage of what we offer, that's okay. We will still enjoy visiting them at family reunions and wedding receptions. They made their choice.

And if they choose our wonderful offer?

Well, our job is to help them.

Yes, we help people … we don't sell people.

We offer people something clearly better than what they currently have, in a way that lets them decide for themselves.

#2: Relax our listener first

We want people to hear our offer:

- Without feeling pressured
- Without feeling judged
- Without feeling rushed
- Without feeling trapped in a sales presentation
- Without feeling we have a sales agenda to close them

Yes, all we want to do is to remove their negative programs and fears and to hear our offer with an open mind.

That's it.

Then, they will hear our offer clearly. Then, they will be able to make a fair decision if what we offer is good for them right now … or not.

This is why we slow things down, remove the feelings of pressure, and make sure our prospects feel in control of the conversation.

When people realize no one is trying to sell them, no one is trying to make their decisions, well, they relax. And that is exactly what we want.

Now, people can hear exactly what we offer without prejudice.

Most people become guarded the moment they sense someone might be trying to "sell" them something. They brace themselves, put up walls, and start looking for "the catch." Their mind closes before we say our first word.

Yikes! That is exactly the opposite of what we want.

We want our listeners to feel our intention is, "No big deal if this option isn't for you."

Step #2 is important.

Skip it, and even our best offers will get rejected.

Think about it. If our listener doesn't believe us, is skeptical, and doesn't trust us, then even if we make the greatest offer ever, we will fail.

#3: Introduce our offer by only talking about the outcome

Huh? No PowerPoint slides? No invitation to a "take a look" opportunity meeting?

Yes. This is not the time for the details. That will come later.

First, people have to make a decision if they want the outcome … or not.

If they don't want the outcome, that is okay. We're done. We can talk about the weather.

If they do want the outcome, then, and only then do we give them the details.

If this feels strange, here is an example.

Imagine someone came to us and said, "So do you want to help me install this oil valve to a pipeline in Turkmenistan?"

We say, "Not really."

Okay. Decision made. Move on. We don't want to hear the entire list of visa details, the newest oil valve regulations, or the current political climate. No need for details!

And if we say, "Yes. I want help install this oil valve to a pipeline in Turkmenistan. I think it would be an exciting travel experience. Can you tell me more details?"

Now it is time to consider what details, how many details, etc. This is where we can do our presentation. And we can make our details as broad or as narrow as we want. The listener is ready to move forward to learn more.

No need to give people the features, the company background, or industry statistics. That can come later, only if they decide they want the outcome.

How can we share our offer? Well, one way is with a small personal story, such as:

"Last year I booked a full week holiday in Hawaii for what I used to pay for three nights. Same resort. Same flights. I just got better pricing."

And then, we can be quiet.

Listeners can make up their minds fast. They either want the same outcome, or not.

Here is the reality.

- We don't start with features
- We don't start with explanations
- We don't start with company details

We start with the outcome.

For example, we share:

- They can save money on trips they already take

- They can travel more often, or more comfortably
- They can stop paying full retail as better options exist
- They can have a part-time income while keeping their jobs
- They can get "paid to travel"
- They can have their dream holidays come true

Now they can decide.

"Does this fit my life right now? Yes or no?"

And, either answer is acceptable.

We are not forcing anything. Instead, we are simply offering an option.

To sum this up, here is the big picture:

1. We know we have something better.
2. We let people relax.
3. We describe the outcome.

They decide if they want the outcome or not.

That's it.

No pressure.

No persuasion tricks.

No awkward conversations.

When people feel respected, good decisions happen. And sometimes their good decision might be, "Not right now."

And this is how we should talk to people about what we offer.

HOW CAN WE HELP LISTENERS RELAX?

We learned in the big picture, Step #1 is to realize that what we offer is better than what our listeners have now. That is easy.

No one wants a smaller bank account.

No one wants to overpay for travel.

But Step #2? "Relax our listener first" … hmmm. We didn't learn that in school. We were too busy memorizing history dates and geometry equations.

A smile helps

Or at the very least, let's not frown. Let's be pleasant.

There is something interesting about smiling. Most people have a program in their brain that says, "If someone smiles, they can be trusted."

Is this program true?

Well, it is true that most people have this program.

But let's remember. Everyone has pre-existing programs in their subconscious minds that may not be 100% accurate all of the time. This is one of them.

Did we ever see a politician smile? Do we ever see a criminal smile?

Of course. We just need to know that if we smile, our chances of success go way up.

But we will have to say something

As soon as we open our mouths, listeners think, "Can I relax and trust what you are saying, or not?"

That's fast. But that is reality. What we say in the first few sentences makes a huge difference.

With friends, or with people who know us, this isn't a challenge. This is easy. But with strangers? Now we have a huge challenge. They don't know us. They are unsure of our intentions. So, in these extreme cases, we will have to say something really good.

Then, what can we say to make sure we don't scare them away? What can we say that will help them relax and open their minds?

How to start with skeptics

Here are plenty of openings that we can choose from. So, if we're stressed, let's pick just one. One that feels natural for us.

At least one of these choices should feel comfortable for us to use when we sense our listener is stressed or skeptical.

"This may or may not be for you."

This is a fast and simple way to take the pressure off listeners. Only 8 words!

And what will our listeners think?

"Oh wow! Thank you. You are not going to try to sell me or force me to do something I don't want to do. And I won't feel obligated to say 'yes' … just to be polite. Okay. Tell me more."

"This is just a peek, not a proposal."

This sentence tells the listeners, "Relax. This isn't a sales presentation. This isn't even all the information you need. This is only enough information to help you decide if you are interested."

We can expect our listeners to let out a sigh of relief.

"Most people love to travel, especially when they can get great bargains, but some people don't want to travel. And that is okay too."

Now our listeners know we are going to talk about travel and travel savings. No secrets. And they can quickly decide if they want more travel in their future, or not. No guilt. No shame. They get to choose their life."

"Only you will know if this feels right or not. Let's take a quick look."

They think, "Only I will know? Yes, that's right! That is how it should be."

"This may or may not be your style. Only you will know for sure."

Hmmm. We just told our listeners that they are in charge. We are not making a decision for them. This relaxes even the most scared skeptics.

More openings that help listeners relax

"It is okay to say 'no', but it is also okay to say 'yes' to this part-time business. You will have to be the one to decide that."

This sentence does something powerful. It gives permission in both directions.

Most people feel trapped when they hear a business opportunity being offered. They worry that saying "no" will offend someone. This sentence removes that fear instantly. There is no obligation to the speaker. They get to choose what is best for them.

This opening also reminds them that saying "yes" is not dangerous or permanent. It's just a choice.

When people feel safe saying "no," they become more open to listening.

"This part-time business is optional. You decide if it fits your life or not."

This sentence puts control exactly where it belongs. With them.

Notice how we appear calm. No urgency. No pressure. No manipulation. Just a simple statement that says, "I trust you to make good decisions for yourself."

That trust is relaxing. They feel our good intentions.

"This isn't for everyone, and that's okay."

This is a strong opening we can use. To some listeners, it feels as though they have to lean forward to qualify. This is attractive to certain types of prospects who are competitive.

And to the non-competitive prospects?

They don't feel like they have to justify their interest or lack of interest. The pressure disappears, and curiosity quietly steps in.

"I am just the messenger, and I know this message isn't for everyone."

This phrase lowers expectations.

We are not positioning ourselves as an expert, a closer, or a persuader. We are simply sharing information. That feels safe. And when people feel safe, they listen longer.

"Using this travel product is entirely up to you. My job is simply to let you know how others have enjoyed it."

This sentence separates information from decision-making.

We are not telling them what to do. We are not telling them what they should want. We share what is working for others. That makes the conversation feel fair and honest.

This gives us a great opening to share our best testimonials.

"I'm not here to convince you … just to share what's working for others."

This line disarms skepticism instantly. Instead of a sales presentation, our listeners expect a story. Everyone loves a good story.

Most people hate being convinced. When they hear this sentence, they relax. They realize we are not trying to win an argument or push them into anything.

"And relax. Your obligation is only to do what is best for your family, not to me."

This is a trust-builder. "Yellow personalities" love it when we talk like this. Love of family is one of their core values.

This sentence tells our listener, "I'm not going to take this personally. I don't know your situation. You do. I am sure you will do what is best for your family."

This opening removes guilt, obligation, and emotional pressure. Our listeners will love that we started with this.

"Your family's needs come first. That is why you should see how this could help."

This sentence aligns us with their priorities, not against them. They now feel like we are a partner, not a salesman.

This opening also helps them to think of something more than just themselves. They might feel more motivated to take a chance if it will help their family's needs.

"I encourage you to look, but the choice to proceed is yours alone."

This phrase encourages curiosity without attachment. Also, this opening is hard to resist. They don't know what we will be offering, so they need a bit more information to decide.

Looking is safe. Deciding can come later. People relax when they realize that we are not forcing them into commitment or action.

"If this works for you, great. If not, that's perfectly fine too."

This sentence removes their fear of making a mistake by not at least listening to this upcoming option.

People don't fear offers. They fear regret. This opening tells the listener that this is something to consider. It might help you. It might not. No pressure.

"Let's skip the presentation and just explore this idea together."

Wow! This is a breath of fresh air.

Nobody likes presentations. Exploring together sounds casual, cooperative, and human. It feels like a conversation, not a sales pitch.

"We already know what ordinary is. This is just an option to not be part of the crowd."

This opening appeals to "red personalities" and "blue personalities." They love to be different. They love to be extraordinary.

We are not saying ordinary is bad. We simply offer an alternative. That feels respectful and intriguing.

And yes, we pushed the curiosity button.

"Think of our part-time business like a menu. You can take what you like and skip the parts you don't like."

This metaphor works because menus feel safe. Everyone can relate to choosing only what they like from a menu.

No pressure. No obligation. No judgment. People instantly understand that they have permission to choose.

"This business (or travel product) isn't for everyone. Just the right people at the right time."

This sentence removes urgency. And, we introduce … timing.

Our listener will think, "Hey, this could be good for me. And if it isn't good for me, I have an automatic excuse. I can say the timing is not right for me at this moment."

"If this helps you, great. If not, maybe you'll know someone it could help."

This lowers resistance even further. Our listeners won't know if this could be good for a friend or not, until they find out more.

Now they don't feel selfish for listening. Even if it's not for them, there's still a reason to pay attention.

"Before I show you how this works, let me tell you what happened to …"

Incoming story!

Our listeners feel safe. We promise a story, and people love stories. This sounds so much better than an incoming sales presentation.

This opening gives us a chance to tell our personal testimonial.

There is no need for skepticism at this point for the listeners. They are only listening to our personal story.

"I don't want you to join, I don't want you to buy, I just want you to look."

This sentence shocks listeners. In a way, this is a nuclear option to overcome intense fear.

When nothing is expected of them, curiosity has room to breathe. And this tells them we won't be "power closing" them into a decision they don't want.

"Nobody is going to ask you to buy, nobody is going to ask you to join. I am only asking you to look."

This opening reinforces safety.

Looking is harmless. Looking is reversible. Looking doesn't require courage or a final decision commitment. Just breathe.

Which one of these openings should I use?

All of these openings have one thing in common: They let people relax and listen with a more open mind.

That is all we ask.

We want people to choose what is best for them. Our mission isn't to manipulate, persuade, or high-pressure someone to do something that is not in their interests.

This is how we let our listeners know we have good intentions for them.

This is how real conversations work.

So which opening feels best and most comfortable for us?

That's up to us! (Yes, we choose.)

We don't have to say all of these openings. Just pick one. Or none.

Our goal is to get our listeners to relax so we can introduce our offer without fear and prejudice.

INTRODUCE OUR OFFER BY ONLY TALKING ABOUT THE OUTCOME

This is where we go to work as professional networkers.

Our job is to help our prospects make a decision.

Now, here is the problem. If we are normal, we carry a bad belief that limits how we talk with people. What is that belief that holds us back?

Belief: People need to understand and know about our offer, BEFORE they can make a decision.

Well … this just isn't true.

Now, we don't have to explain or give our prospects details and information. They will want to make up their minds, yes or no, by just knowing what the outcome will be.

If the outcome is something they are interested in?

They will reply, "Yes. I would like that. Can you now give me the details?"

If the outcome is something they are not interested in?

They will change the subject and want to talk about something else. Their decision is that the outcome we described is not important to them now.

If this seems strange, no problem. Later, we will look at many examples that will prove to us that people make decisions before the information.

But for now, let's look at something practical we can use immediately.

Tiny questions

Can we memorize two sentences?

Here are the two sentences:

1. **"Do you have this problem?"**

2. **"Would it be okay if you could fix it?"**

The first sentence asks our prospects, "Is there something you are missing in your life? Do you wish you had something you don't have now? Is there a problem that bothers you?"

If our prospects say, "Yes" … we will then ask the second question:

"Would it be okay if you could fix it?"

Who knows? Maybe our prospects want to fix their problem, maybe not. That is their choice. We are just checking.

So, what happens when our prospects agree that they have a problem that they want to fix? They want to know how to fix it. Now it's time for the details.

So, as we see, details come later.

Without going too deep into this, let's do some practical examples. Once we see these examples, we will feel great about talking to people. Ready?

Q. "Do you like taking holidays?"

Q. "Would it be okay if you could do it for half price?"

Q. "Do you save a little bit every month for your annual holiday?"

Q. "Would it be okay if your monthly deposits got you even better deals?"

Q. "Do you know other people who like to take holidays?"

Q. "Would it be okay if you got paid because they travel?"

Q. "Do you like to take cruises?"

Q. "Would it be okay if you could get extra discounts, or even go for free?"

Q. "Do you like to travel?"

Q. "Would it be okay if you could travel at wholesale or discounted rates instead?"

Q. "Do you hate Mondays?"

Q. "Would it be okay if you got an extra paycheck so you could have 3-day weekends forever?"

Q. "Do you like taking holidays?"

Q. "Would it be okay if you got paid even while taking your holidays?"

Q. "Do you like saving money and getting bargains?"

Q. "Would it be okay if you got great bargains when you take your holidays?"

Q. "Do you ever feel like travel costs keep going up every year?"

Q. "Would it be okay if you had access to better travel that actually goes down in price, instead of up in price?"

Q. "Do you ever look at trips and think, 'Maybe next year'?"

Q. "Would it be okay if 'next year' became this year instead?"

Q. "Do you enjoy nice hotels, but not the prices?"

Q. "Would it be okay if you could stay in better places for less money?"

Q. "Do you ever feel guilty spending money on travel?"

Q. "Would it be okay if your trips felt like smart bargains instead of wasted money?"

Q. "Do you like the idea of upgrading your travel without upgrading your budget?"

Q. "Would it be okay if you could make this happen on your next holiday?"

Q. "Do you already book your personal holidays online like most people?"

Q. "Would it be okay if you simply paid less for doing the same travel plans?"

Q. "Do you know people who complain about the cost of travel?"

Q. "Would it be okay if you had something helpful to show them?"

Q. "Do you ever hear about great travel deals other people found?"

Q. "Would it be okay if you were the one getting the deals first?"

Q. "Do you enjoy planning trips?"

Q. "Would it be okay if you had more travel options instead of fewer?"

Q. "Do you feel like vacations go by too fast?"

Q. "Would it be okay if you could take them more often?"

Q. "Do you like helping friends when you find something useful?"

Q. "Would it be okay if helping your friends also helped you?"

Q. "Do you like the idea of an extra paycheck every month?"

Q. "Would it be okay if you got these checks regularly?"

Q. "Do you think paying less is better than paying more for travel?"

Q. "Would it be okay if you could get discounts for your travel in the future?"

And now the magic appears

Are we feeling the trend with these questions?

This is something we can do from day one. Simply ask two questions and take the … **volunteers!**

No selling. No convincing. No rejection.

We only continue the conversation with the people who want to know more.

Yes, when people tell us they want the outcome, this means we will only give the details to people who have already said "yes" to our offer.

Why do these questions feel good?

Because they work. We get to the point.

At this point in the conversation, our prospects don't want to know:

- The background of the company
- Who founded the company
- How this system works
- What is the compensation plan
- What is the money commitment

At this point, early in our conversation, our prospects only want to know if the outcome is something they want or not.

No one is interested in the details, unless they are interested in the outcome. We will save a lot of time for ourselves and our prospects by focusing on the outcome.

The very first decision people make is:

"Do I want this outcome or not?"

And this is the biggest decision we must get as professional networkers.

Will my prospects change their decisions after I give them the details?

Sometimes. Remember, we are only giving the details to people who want the outcome.

Maybe some of our prospects find out they don't have a passport for their dream travel yet. Maybe finances are tight for now, but they will be better later. Or maybe they got fired from their job this morning, and they have other things on their minds right now. It happens.

But for most of our prospects, they will be excited to learn the details.

Think about this from our prospects' point of view.

When we give details to people who want the outcome, they will be looking for reasons why this will work for them, instead of reasons why it won't work for them.

This is different than the old-time selling from the 1980s.

Old-time selling insisted on giving people details and information first. While the pushy salesman was wasting time with detail overload, what were the prospects thinking?

They were probably thinking, "Let me look for reasons why not. I will need some negative reasons to prevent this pushy salesman from trying to close me at the end of his stupid sales presentation."

People don't decide based on information and details

They decide based on the outcome.

The information and details come after the big decision.

Will the information and details delay or disqualify some of the people who want the outcome? Yes.

But many will want the outcome as we describe the information and details.

Remember. We are taking the volunteers. And this feels good.

This chapter is not about memorizing questions

It's about learning to:

- Slow down

- Respecting our listeners' time
- Let listeners think for themselves
- Let listeners choose
- Let curiosity do the work

When we talk about outcomes, we remove pressure. We are not convincing. We are not pushing our agenda.

Instead, when we remove pressure, our listeners relax.

When listeners relax, they listen.

And when they listen, they decide clearly without feeling manipulated or sold to.

That's how professionals network.

Our prospects want to know the outcome before they decide to set aside time to learn the details. When we respect these wishes, wow!

We will only talk to the … volunteers!

There are many other ways we can talk to others that we will learn, but before we do, let's reinforce an important lesson.

DECISIONS FIRST: DETAILS LATER

This is the hardest belief we must change to make our business better.

If we truly believe that people make instant decisions, then our businesses will feel full of joy and fun.

If we hold onto our old beliefs that people need information to make a decision, we will feel like pushy salespeople and invite constant rejection.

But how do we change our long-held beliefs?

The easiest way to change our beliefs is through personal experiences and observing real-life situations.

Let's start now.

Here are 14 case studies that will help us change our beliefs about how people make decisions. Many of these are taken from a book I wrote long ago about how humans make decisions.

People don't wait for lightning to strike their brains. They don't wait for mysterious voices from the clouds. And most of all, we don't make decisions by weighing 4,000 reasons for ... and 3,900 reasons against.

No.

We make decisions instantly … on almost no information.

But don't take someone's word for it. Instead, look at these case studies and feel what is happening in real-world experiences.

CASE STUDY #1:

Jorge and I conduct a training. We announce to the attendees, "When we finish today, we are going to get ice cream. Who wants to come with us?"

Over half the attendees raise their hands.

They made their decision instantly, before they heard the details.

Details?

"Where is the ice cream place? Is it local or far away? How many flavors do they have? Will Jorge and Big Al pay for everyone's ice cream, or will we have to pay for our own? Does this ice cream place have a website? Who is the owner of the ice cream place?"

Nope. The details didn't matter. The decision was instant. Over half of the attendees made a "yes" decision in seconds.

What about those who made a "no" decision? What were they thinking?

"I'm lactose intolerant. I'm not hungry. I must hurry home to relieve our babysitter. My favorite sports team is playing on television in 30 minutes. I don't even like ice cream."

And, this trip for ice cream is not for them. And that is okay.

CASE STUDY #2:

You and I are hungry. We walk past several restaurants and finally go inside a cute restaurant to eat. We chose a table. Order drinks. Look at the menu. Get appetizers. Order the main course. And yes, we get dessert.

Finally, the bill comes. Now here is the question.

"When did we make our final decision to eat at this restaurant?"

Yes! Before we even choose where to sit!

Looks like we made a decision before the details.

CASE STUDY #3:

Let's say we take our family to a nice restaurant to celebrate a birthday. We decide to order the chicken entrée. But did we ask, "Are the vegetables grown organically under natural light? What about that chicken? Did my chicken live a happy life before it was killed?"

We don't know. However, we made our final decision to purchase that entrée without a fact-filled presentation. Hmmm.

CASE STUDY #4:

Did we ever get an unplanned telephone call from a salesman? Ugh!

How many seconds into the telephone conversation before we make our final decision?

Most times, we make a "no" decision before the salesman finishes his first sentence. We make our final decision before the presentation even starts! And guess what?

Now, if we make our final decision with a salesman over the telephone in just seconds … uh oh! Wait!

Don't we think our prospects will do the same to us when we talk with them? What percentage of the time? Almost 100%!

CASE STUDY #5:

Did we ever go food shopping at a huge supermarket?

We push our cart down aisle four. On the left is a box of cornflakes. Do we stop our cart, pick up the box of cornflakes, and read the nutrition label? Do we check the background of the company founder? Do we review the financials of the cornflake company? Do we consider the lost opportunity cost of eating cornflakes rather than doing some productive work?

No. We make an instant decision to bypass the cornflakes and continue down the aisle.

If we stop and consider every item in this aisle, and then get a full presentation on each item, we would starve before we reached the end of the first aisle.

Instead, how do we proceed down that grocery store aisle? We do this. Mentally, we say, "No. No. No. Yes to that chocolate bar. Yes to that giant bag of cookies. No. No. Yes to that cake. No. No."

We have pre-made decisions on almost every item in the grocery store.

Again, decision before details. Hmmm.

CASE STUDY #6:

Imagine someone comes up to us and says, "I just took my first lesson to become a chiropractor. I learned a brand-new technique on how to twist your neck. Do you want to be first? I need the practice."

In one second, we make our final decision. We think, "No. I want to survive. This sounds too dangerous. No. No. No."

We make that immediate decision before we hear the details of the presentation. Before we hear that he saw this technique on the Internet. Before he tells us that 30% of the people could recover. Before he shows us his most recent test grades.

Our uninformed decision happens fast.

CASE STUDY #7:

Imagine a stranger approaches us and says, "Can I take your children skydiving with me?"

Now, depending on what our children did to us while they were growing up, we would think, "Oh no! Please don't take my babies skydiving!" or "I would help push them out of the plane!"

Assuming we love our children, our immediate answer would be, "No."

How long did it take us to make that final decision? It was instant. We have an internal program called "love of family."

Notice that we made our final decision before he even started his skydiving presentation? Before he told us that he was a professional skydiver? Before he told us that he was successful three out of four times? Before he told us that we would only dive one centimeter?

Yes, we make decisions before the details and the presentation.

CASE STUDY #8:

Let's talk politics.

In ten days, the leader of the opposing political party is set to give a speech. He will address our nation on how he plans to fix all the current problems.

Now, have we already made a decision? Have we already decided it will just be some political gibberish and fluff from the opposing political party's twisted viewpoint?

Of course. But think about this.

We made our final decision about his speech instantly … but he won't even begin his speech for ten more days!

Whoa!!!

We made our final decision … ten days before the speech ever happened! This politician didn't have a chance.

CASE STUDY #9:

We call a friend and say, "Let's meet for coffee on Tuesday morning. I want to tell you about a new business you and I can do. You will like it."

Our friend agrees.

What happens on Tuesday morning? Our friend doesn't show up. He didn't even have the manners to tell us that he wasn't coming.

Did our friend already make a decision? Yes. He made a "no" decision based on … no real information. Oh.

But what if our friend shows up with a smile on his face?

Hint!

Our friend has made a decision that he wants a business. He decided to sneak out of work, skip his coffee break, and take time out of his busy day to meet with us.

Our friend's decision was made before the appointment.

CASE STUDY #10:

The ladies' shoe store. A young lady walks into a large shoe store. Over 1,000 pairs of ladies' shoes on display. But next door is a ladies' shoe store with a 95%-off sale!

How long will this young lady stay in the original shoe store? Seconds.

She will make an instant "no" decision on 1,000 pairs of ladies' shoes, just so that she can run to the next store with that incredible 95%-off sale.

Did we notice that this lady did not receive a single presentation on the original 1,000 pairs of shoes? No salesman told her about the quality of the Italian leather, about the little old shoemaker who lived up in the mountains, that the shoemaker's son walked with a crutch, the reinforced shoe buckles, the history of the styling, how someone cut the original leather from a favorite cow's hide, etc.

Fast decisions happen … a lot!

CASE STUDY #11:

A man sits in front of the television mindlessly channel-surfing. The remote control goes, "Click. Click. Click. Click." After two seconds of viewing a channel, the man changes to the next channel.

This behavior drives his wife crazy. She wonders, "How can he make a decision to watch that channel or not? He hasn't seen anything yet! Men are so stupid!"

But the reality? Men make their final decision to continue surfing channels until they find the channel that instantly grabs their interest.

CASE STUDY #12:

At live workshops, I ask this question of the ladies:

"Ladies, have you ever, sometime in your lifetime, met a young man, made up your mind about that young man, and where that young man would fit into your life, and made that decision within the first 30 seconds of meeting that young man?"

The ladies smile and say, "Yes."

Then, I ask the men at the workshop, "Is this fair?"

Of course, the men scream, "This is not fair! The ladies have not heard our sales presentation yet!"

But the ladies will say, "Sorry. That is how it works in real life."

Reality is reality.

Decisions are fast.

CASE STUDY #13:

At the same live workshop, I want to be fair. So, I ask this question of the entire audience:

"How many people here have made their final decision to enter a relationship, or even get married … before they had all the information?"

After some uncomfortable laughs, the audience agrees that we make our final decisions instantly. The information does not come until much later.

CASE STUDY #14:

Try this. Let's go online. Let's pick a random video to watch.

How many seconds does it take us to make our final decision … if we want to watch this video or not?

Five seconds? Ten seconds?

We make our final decision before we see the entire video!

Are we starting to see a trend?

Yeah. It is obvious.

The big decision is, "Do we want the outcome … or not?"

It doesn't take long for that decision to happen.

But here is the exciting news!

This means we don't have to worry much about a "sales presentation" or explaining details.

We are not some salesmen trying to manipulate or convince our listeners. We only talk with the volunteers who want what we offer.

So let's stop sweating about the PowerPoint presentation, when to show a company video, or tricking someone to show up to a surprise sales presentation.

That isn't us.

We know the reality.

"Our listeners know if they want our outcome, or not"

If they want our outcome, then everything else will flow naturally. We can answer questions, show only the details they want, and not be worried that we have to "sell" someone on the complete details and facts.

If they don't want the outcome we offer, that is okay. We can still be friends. We can still go to the family reunion together. We will simply choose to talk about something else with our non-interested listener.

MORE STEP #3 ICEBREAKERS

Remember the big picture?

#1: What we offer is better than what they have now.

Okay, this one is easy.

#2: Relax our listener first.

We learn a lot of relaxing opening word phrases and sentences that will relax our prospects and open their minds.

#3: Introduce our offer by only talking about the outcome.

Remember those tiny questions that we could start with? For example:

"Do you like to travel? Would it be okay if you could pay less for your travel?"

Let's create more "icebreakers" to introduce our travel and business offers

The definition of an "icebreaker" is something we can say to take our conversation from social chit-chat … to talking about a great business offer.

Using tiny questions is only one version of an icebreaker. There are so many more that we can learn.

Having many icebreakers is so much fun. If we have a big inventory of great things to say, we can pick the perfect opening for almost any prospect, in any situation.

This next icebreaker formula is powerful. Why?

#1. Because there is no rejection. It is so safe that even the shyest people can use it.

#2. This icebreaker formula never feels pushy. We won't feel like we are taking advantage of relationships.

#3: We get instant decisions using this icebreaker. By now, we should understand that getting instant decisions is the secret weapon to success in our network marketing business.

Instant decisions?

Yes. Remember the last chapter?

People make fast decisions if they want the outcome we describe.

When we can get fast "yes" decisions, 95% of our work is done.

This fast instant decision is not the finish line, but we are almost there. Our prospects are on our side. At this point, we answer easy questions and share any details they want. This is minor stuff.

The big job is done. Getting that "yes" decision.

And don't worry about questions and details now. That is minor. We'll talk about that later.

So, for now, let's learn the next icebreaker formula.

BENEFIT + PERMISSION

Yes. That is the entire formula.

"Benefit + Permission."

Simple. Easy to learn. Something we can use the very first day we are in this business.

When appropriate in a conversation, we will announce a business benefit that our listeners might want. And then, we give our listeners permission to raise their hands and say:

"I really like that benefit. That is something I want in my life. How do I get it? Can you explain it to me? What are the details?"

Okay, they won't ask exactly like that, but we get the idea. We mention a great benefit, and they tell our listeners it is okay to ask us for more details.

But let's think about this for just one moment.

Nobody asks for more details about something they don't want!

The only listeners who ask us for more details are the listeners who make the mental "yes" decision, that they want the benefit.

This will become apparent in the examples.

Our listeners feel safe. The conversation feels natural.

Our listeners can ignore the benefit we offer and talk about something else.

They can also want our benefit.

It is their choice.

No pressure.

No pitching.

No hard selling.

Our listeners feel in control and never threatened. They love it.

There are only two steps, two things to learn, so let's get started.

Step #1: Find a benefit that we love about our business

This is so easy. We love talking about our benefits. Benefits are everywhere! Let's make a small list of travel benefits now.

- Paying less for trips you already take
- Traveling more often for less money
- Staying in five-star hotels for two-star prices
- Cruising for less, or even free
- Taking vacations without guilt
- Earning while you travel
- Turning travel expenses into tax advantages
- Dream holidays instead of ordinary holidays
- Vacations that are worth 1,000 pictures
- Paying wholesale or insider rates instead of retail
- Upgrading rooms, views, or cabins without upgrading the price
- Traveling when you want, not just when prices are low
- Turning "maybe someday" trips into "this year" trips
- More flexibility with destinations and dates

- Access to travel options most people never see
- Less stress planning trips
- Feeling smart instead of guilty about spending on travel
- Traveling like a local, not like a tourist
- Access to spontaneous getaway bargains
- Making memories instead of just taking time off
- Giving your family experiences instead of more stuff
- The whole family can travel at affordable prices
- Having something exciting on the calendar all year
- Traveling with confidence instead of price anxiety
- Turning referrals into travel credits or income
- Never overpaying full retail "just because" again
- Having travel stories worth telling (and retelling)
- Feeling rewarded for travel instead of punished by prices
- Living a dream people say they want, but never plan for

Okay, enough benefits? Can we think of more? Of course, but we now think in benefits, the ultimate outcome our listeners will hear from us.

Remember, listeners only want the outcome first. If they like the outcome, they will ask us to tell them more. That is when we can give them whatever details they want.

Step #2: Give our prospects "permission" to ask us more if they are interested

This is where the magic happens in this icebreaker formula.

Asking permission removes pressure and gives control to our listeners. When our listeners feel in control, they relax. When they relax, they listen without a lot of prejudice or fear of being sold.

That's why this formula works so well.

We allow our listeners to volunteer, to raise their hands, only if they want to hear more. And because our benefits and outcomes are so compelling, most listeners will want to hear more.

But … asking permission? How do I give them permission?

Easy. Here are some phrases we could use:

- Would you like to know my plan?
- Would you like to know what I am doing?
- Would you like to know his secret?
- Would you like to know what she did?
- Would you like to know how it works?

These little permission questions make this comfortable for us. We don't feel pushy. We don't appear needy.

These little permission questions make our listeners so relaxed. They feel comfortable talking to us. They appreciate that they get to make the choice to continue the conversation or not.

And this comfort level is why the icebreaker formula works. No rejection. No bad feelings. And we never feel that we are selling or taking advantage of a friendship. Instead, we feel like we are helping others by giving them one more option for their lives.

When do we say this benefits + permission icebreaker?

Here are some examples of announcing a benefit, and then asking permission if our prospects want to know more.

First, let's establish a good rapport. Give our prospects a chance to talk first. Encourage them to talk about something that added value to their lives or some new development.

Us: "What is new with you?"

Prospect talks and then asks us: "What is new with you?"

We have rapport. We are in conversation. We politely listened to our prospect. And now our prospect asks us, "What is new with you?"

Time for our icebreaker answer.

Let's put this formula to use

Step #1 (benefit): "I now get better vacations than before, and at a lower price too."

Step #2: (permission): "Would you like to know how I do it?"

Done!

Step back. Breathe. Allow our listeners to decide if they want to get better vacations and lower prices, also. Or, our listeners could decide, "Oh no. Not for me. I pride myself on overpaying. I flunked math in school. Please don't let me know how I can improve my life!"

Okay. A bit over the top. But almost everyone will want us to tell them more. Easy. Rejection-free. Our listeners are excited to know more.

Isn't this what we want?

Our listeners have made a decision that they want the outcome!

This is huge. No closing. Nothing. Our listeners volunteered to know more. They have made a "yes" decision that they want what we offer.

This is 95% of our work. The remaining 5%?

Giving details about how this works to our listeners.

We don't have to give many details. Only the details our listeners want. They can learn more later if they want.

But for now, we have our listeners on our side. They want the same things we have. Explaining is easy. We are talking to a friend, not some skeptical stranger that we are trying to convince.

This feels great!

More examples

When our benefit + permission icebreakers work, listeners will say, "Tell me more."

We made it easy for them to say "yes" and to ask more about our benefit.

What happens if our prospects are not interested?

They can change the subject and talk about the weather, sports, or shopping. This is what happens in all conversations. We change topics often.

So relax. Have fun. Take the volunteers.

Here are more examples for us to use.

- "I get a lot of free travel credits every month. Would you like to know how I get them?"

- "My sister showed me how to take five-star holidays for budget prices. Would you like to know what she showed me?"

- "Looks like I'll be able to travel more and still spend less money this year. Would you like to know how that's happening?"

- "My travel costs keep going down instead of up. Would you like to know why?"

- "I stopped paying full retail for hotels. Would you like to know how that works?"

- "I can book my same trips as before, but now for less money. Would you like to see how I do this?"

- "I've been upgrading my travel without upgrading my budget. Would you like to know what I'm using?"

- "We found a way to travel more often on the same budget. Would you like to know how my wife and I do it?"

- "I can now plan trips without stressing about cost. Would you like to know my secret?"

- "Looks like I have enough credits for another free cruise. Would you like to know how I get them?"

- "I save money every month for my annual holiday. Now I can make that money multiply and go further. Would you like to know my plan?"

We can think of hundreds of good icebreaker openings for our travel business. The good news is that this formula is simple. We can create and customize our benefit + permission conversation starters so that we can deliver the best outcome that a listener might want.

Remember, let's not have a pushy sales agenda. Let's allow our listeners to decide if now is the right time in their lives to take advantage of this outcome … or not.

If our listeners are not interested, they will give us a polite hint. They will change the subject to sports, food, children, the news, politics … or whatever else is more interesting to them.

And that is okay. This isn't their time.

We don't have to sell, convince, or persuade them. There are so many people desperately wanting the outcomes we offer. Let's just work with the volunteers for now.

We only offer an option. We are not demanding that our listeners take action. Breathe. Relax. Enjoy the conversations.

But ... what about my business opportunity?

Yes, this same formula works for offering our business opportunity to others.

Let's start with Step #1: Benefits.

Ready to make a list?

- Work from home
- Fire the boss
- More time with the children
- Two paychecks instead of one paycheck
- Give ourselves a raise
- No more commuting
- Make travel a tax deduction
- Become our own boss

- Be a business owner, not an employee
- A chance to earn big money
- Enjoy my work
- Getting paid what I am worth
- Earn money when my friends travel
- I don't have 100% of my income depending on the mood swing of my boss
- Earn part-time until I grow into full-time
- Build something that grows beyond just my effort
- Have control of my day schedule
- Can earn more than my friends who went to university
- Earn based on my results, no politics
- Low startup risks, not like a traditional business
- Can fit my work around my family's schedule
- Work with positive people, not coffee-break complainers
- Get paid on performance instead of seniority
- I can work from anywhere with Wi-Fi
- I never have to beg permission for time off

This should be enough benefits to start. We can always add more.

Let's now add some permission phrases and admire our new icebreakers. Ready?

- "I can work from wherever I happen to be traveling. Would you like to hear how I set that up?"

- "I'm turning some of my trips into tax-advantaged expenses now. Would you like to know how I learned that?"

- "I used to travel. Now I get paid to travel. Would you like to know my secret?"

- "I never have to ask for vacation time off. Would you like to know what changed?"

- "I get a small raise every month. Would you like to know how that works?"

- "Looks like I won't have to commute to work ever again. Would you like to know my secret plan?"

- "My neighbor works out of his home full-time now. Would you like to know how he does it?"

- "I've got a plan that will give me three-day weekends forever. Would you like to know my plan?"

- "I got two Christmas bonuses this year. Would you like to know what happened?"

- "My wife now earns more money part-time than her boss does full-time. Would you like to know how she does it?"

- Us: "I got a secret plan to escape from this job. Would you like to hear my plan during coffee break?"

- "I'm building a paycheck that travels with me wherever I go. Would you like to know what I do?"

Oh my! And we are only starting. Making these icebreakers is fun.

How about a little creativity?

"Everyone hates my neighbor. Every morning, she sits on her front steps, sips her coffee, and waves goodbye to everyone going to work. Would you like to know her secret how she can just stay home and smile?"

Okay. These benefit + permission icebreaker conversation starters work. All we do now is … stop talking.

Our listeners can decide if they are interested or not. If they want the outcome we offered, or not.

- We are no longer chasing people.
- We are no longer explaining too much.
- We are letting curiosity do the work.
- We are letting our listeners make … instant decisions!

We don't need to memorize all of these icebreakers.

Just choose one or two that excite us. Yes, pick what feels comfortable for us.

One final example to make sure we stay on track

At our job on Monday, we can say this to a co-worker:

Step #1 (benefit): "Looks like I can quit my job at the end of the year."

Step #2 (permission): "Would you like to know my plan?"

Our co-worker pleads, "Yes! Don't leave here without me. Tell me now!"

Us: "Well, we can't talk now. We're on our job. Maybe we could chat during our coffee break or on Saturday."

Co-worker: "I can't wait. Tell me now!"

Do we see where this conversation is going? This is a fun way to offer a great outcome to others.

And one final word about posture

When we offer an outcome without a sales agenda, we show power. We show the confidence we have in what we offer.

Listeners sense our sincerity. They sense we want to help. They sense that we have their best interests at heart.

We are okay if today is not their day. We are okay if they never want the outcomes we offer. They feel honored that we trust them to make their own decisions for their lives.

Why can we feel so confident?

Because there are so many people desperate for the outcomes we offer. We don't have to be for everyone. There will be plenty of volunteers for us when we offer great outcomes.

SOUNDBITES

Nervous? Can't think of what to say? Here is a shortcut.

Soundbites to the rescue.

What is a soundbite?

Simple. Just a short phrase or sentence that sticks in people's brains. Maybe it forms an image in their brains that they can't get out. Maybe it touches a deep emotional need.

But the true power of a soundbite is this. It triggers an immediate "yes" decision.

Why do soundbites work?

Because our listeners have short attention spans. When we talk, are people listening to us? Or, are they busy with their own thoughts? Ouch!

It is like our listeners are in some sort of hypnotic trance. They pretend to listen, but our message goes in one ear and, of course, out the other ear.

The reality is this. When we talk, only a tiny percentage of what we say will be remembered. Let's make sure we say something interesting that will stick in our listeners' minds and help them see our awesome offers.

What is an example of a sound bite?

"Finger-Lickin' Good" (KFC)

We remember this. This is simple and vivid in our minds. And the next time we see a KFC restaurant, we might replay in our minds the words, "Finger-Licking Good."

This is the power of a clear benefit or outcome. It's memorable. And the best part?

We can use these soundbite phrases and sentences anywhere in our conversations. They are great for prospecting, icebreakers, presentations, and even to get referrals.

But enough about the soundbite benefits, let's make a starting list of soundbites we could use. Ready?

Travel soundbites

"Get paid to vacation."

"Trade your alarm clock for a sunrise at sea."

"Five-star travel on a three-star budget."

"I am turning my bucket list into a 'been there' list."

"Stop vacationing at your mother-in-law's apartment with her 32 cats."

"Born to travel?"

"Send postcards to your co-workers from Hawaii."

"I like working from a beach instead of a cubicle."

"I didn't want to just dream about it. I wanted to post about it."

"I want to collect moments, not things."

"Live for more than just weekends!"

"Travel like an insider, not a tourist."

"How to pay wholesale prices for a retail lifestyle."

"Why pay full price when you can pay 'friend' price?"

"Travel more for less than you spend on coffee."

"Life is more than the inside of an office."

"Don't waste your vacation days on ordinary vacations."

"I'd rather have a passport full of stamps than a house full of stuff."

"Travel now, because 'someday' isn't a day of the week."

"Friends don't let friends stay home."

"Wake up in a new time zone."

"Activate vacation mode: Permanently!"

"Get upgraded to first class without the first-class price tag."

"Travel like a local, live like a king."

"The secret menu of the travel industry."

"Retire early, travel often."

"Trading the morning commute for a morning dip."

"Make your 'Out of Office' reply … permanent."

"Earn while you explore the world."

"Don't just watch the Travel Channel. Live it in person."

"I was one fluorescent light away from a meltdown."

"Because 'staycation' is just another word for 'doing laundry.'"

"Vacations that cost less than staying home."

"I stopped collecting souvenirs. Now I collect boarding passes."

"Travel prices so low they feel like a typo."

"The only thing I pay full price for now is airport coffee."

"My favorite hobby requires a passport."

"I go places that I used to just 'like' on Instagram."

Okay, now we have better words to say to get our offers inside our listeners' minds.

These soundbites don't require perfect timing, perfect delivery, or perfect confidence. They work because they are simple and memorable.

We don't have to give our listeners unlimited information. Sometimes, one unforgettable idea is all they need to make their decisions.

WHAT TO SAY NEXT? FOUR WORDS!

Here is the short story with the four words. We'll examine why these four words work in a moment.

Here are the four words:

"Then, we should talk."

That's it. And then stop speaking.

Allow our listener to pick a time to discuss this more. That time could be right now, at a more convenient or more appropriate time.

When we say, "Then, we should talk" … this shows confidence to our listeners, not desperation. Desperation is never attractive.

What do we mean by desperation? We could answer our listeners' requests for more information by panicking and saying:

- "You have to set an appointment before I can give you the details."
- "You have to watch this 35-minute video."
- "Let me dump my sales pitch on you now."
- "Shut up and let me explain everything quickly before you change your mind!"

Okay. We're not going to be this extreme, but we got the idea. Relax, and our listeners will also relax.

If we rush, we:

- Create pressure
- Trigger skepticism
- Sound rehearsed

When we say, "Then, we should talk", we show respect for our listeners' time. They feel they are in control. They are choosing the pace and feel more comfortable with us.

After we give our benefit + permission icebreaker, we can expect most people to think, "Yeah, this is an outcome I want. How does this work? I am curious about the details."

The big decision has been made. They want what we have to offer.

But most listeners will have questions and need some details. Some will need more details, and a few won't need details at all. We just try to help.

More about how to describe the details a bit later. But for now, let's stay focused.

When we explain the details, our listeners will feel better. Even though they want the outcome we described, they may have situations holding them back. That's life. Well, it is their lives, and we are not responsible for their current situation.

What situations could prevent listeners from taking advantage of the outcomes we described?

- Death in the family
- Bad finances
- Self-sabotaging subconscious mind programs
- Complications at work

- Current personal drama

Stuff happens in life. There will never be a perfect time for 100% of the people we talk to. This is why we understand why some listeners could later change their minds after we pass on the details.

Remember, we are only offering an option to improve our listeners' lives. That's it. Today could be their day, or not.

The big benefit

When we say, "Then, we should talk" … our listeners pick the best time for our chat. We are not begging for an appointment. There is no pressure. Our listeners can pick the time, the place, and how long they have for the details.

Some listeners want to hear some details immediately. Others, later in the day. And some, later in the week, when they are in a more relaxing environment. They get to choose.

But oh, it gets better.

What if we were just messaging someone?

We don't want to give the details and presentation by text. So when we say, "Then, we should talk" … we direct the conversation to an audio or video call, or even a face-to-face visit.

In-person conversations are the best. So much is lost in text.

And speaking of online, let's look at that now.

BUT WHAT ABOUT ONLINE POSTING AND MESSAGING?

This should be easy for us now. We know the basics.

Here is an old marketing rule that keeps us from overselling:

"The purpose of an ad is to get a phone call."

The message? Don't try to sell by posting and messaging. Don't try to convince and educate by posting and messaging.

Instead, create curiosity. Invite a personal conversation.

Just to be clear.

1. Posting or advertising should not be the entire sales presentation. Instead, the purpose of most posts and advertisements is to motivate the reader to contact us. We can then take it from there.

2. Messaging is nice, but terrible for selling and explaining what we offer. We want to motivate people to want to have a conversation with us. The phrase, "Then, we should talk" … is a great way to get off the keyboard and into a voice conversation.

Of course, this is in a perfect world. It doesn't always work out, but we try.

Why text-based messaging is challenging

- There are no smiles.

- No body language.

- No friendly tone of voice.

- They can't see a picture of our family or pets.

And without these clues, we remain a dangerous stranger to others. There is a natural resistance.

This is exactly why the Benefit + Permission formula works so well online. It keeps conversations light, optional, and human.

Online, shorter is better. We are not trying to:

- Impress

- Educate

- Convince

- Explain

We are checking for one thing.

"Is this outcome interesting to you?"

That's it.

If the outcome is interesting, then we should talk.

Easy.

How do we check with an icebreaker conversation starter?

Well, the good news is that we will learn many types of icebreakers and formulas. Here are just a few examples. And remember, people make fast decisions. That is why these work so well.

"A quick question. Do you enjoy travel and holidays?"

If they say "yes" … we will continue.

"I found a way to travel more and get better holidays for a lot less money. Would you like to know what I found?" (If they say yes, we would say this.)

"Then, we should talk."

And if they say "no" … or are not interested, we finish the conversation or talk about something else. No need for drama. No need to push. No need to make them feel guilty. No awkwardness. No chasing.

What we have is good. We will take the volunteers. There will be plenty of volunteers in our future who want what we offer.

"My part-time business saves me on travel, and I even get paid to travel. Would you like to know how this works?" (For yes replies, we would say this.)

"Then, we should talk."

More examples of getting yes replies?

"I can now travel at wholesale instead of retail. Would you like to know how it works?"

"Then, we should talk. Are you online now?"

"Would it be okay if you could travel more, but pay far less for your travel expenses?"

"Then, we should talk."

No pressure.

No urgency.

No selling.

Instead …

Short.

Friendly.

Optional.

This is fun. We can enjoy prospecting when we make great offers and only take the volunteers.

But what about some interesting post ideas that sort out volunteers? A post where only the most interested people respond? We could say:

"I am working on getting even more free travel and holidays. Not for everyone, but if you like traveling and holidays, message me. We'll figure out a time to talk."

"Do you have an annoying job? Ever dream about a career in travel? I'm happy to tell you how I did it."

"My body was made for cruising. Now, I am even getting paid to cruise. Want a part-time income with cruise benefits? Message me, and we'll set up a time to chat."

Some online reminders

Our online success is not about saying more.

It's about saying less, but saying it better.

- One benefit
- No pressure
- Presenting our benefit as an option
- A permission question
- And the discipline to stop talking

Why are we being so brief?

Because online attention is fragile and short. People quickly judge whether they want the outcome or not.

While every contact is unique, here are some general guidelines for things we should avoid.

- Long explanations. We haven't earned their attention span yet.
- Boring, chatty, voice notes. No one wants to listen to a recorded sales pitch.
- PDFs with details of things we are not interested in at this moment.
- Links to more information. More information is not what they are looking for.
- Dumping people off to a company video, which is little more than a commercial.

We're not asking for commitment.

We're not asking for time.

We're not asking for belief.

We're only asking one small question. And that question is:

"Is this outcome interesting to you?"

If yes, we can continue. And smile.

If not, we can move on. And smile.

We can make our travel careers fun!

THE DETAILS

Remember the big picture?

#1: What we offer is better than what they have now

#2: Relax our listener first

#3: Introduce our offer by only talking about the outcome

This is 95% of our business.

Once we introduce our offer, listeners make an instant decision if they want the outcome or not.

The remaining 5% of our business?

Sharing and explaining any details our listeners wish to know. And this part is easy. No selling. No convincing. No persuading.

Our listeners want what we offer. They want us to support their decision and answer questions about how to move forward.

Well, how do we answer the details for our listeners?

The good news is that we don't have to overthink this. We do the best we can.

Remember, our listeners have already made a "yes" decision. We now have a common goal.

Some listeners will want every detail imaginable! Yikes! Well, okay then. We will try to give them everything they need.

Other listeners won't want any details. They want to start now. Let's not hold them back.

And most listeners? They will want some details. Some will want to know how they can earn money part-time. Others want to know how long it will take them to qualify for a free trip.

Well, if our listeners want to know different details, then how will we know what to talk about so that we don't bore them?

Easy.

Two strategies

#1. Give a quick overview. Now they can direct us to the details they want us to explain.

#2. Ask them directly, "What would you like to know first?"

This is a conversation, not a sales pitch. Our listeners want to know some details because they want to:

- See if they can afford this
- See how much they can save
- Understand how they can earn free trips
- Be sure to avoid a big obligation
- Know if they have the skills to take advantage of this business
- Know if someone will train them on what they don't know
- Explain this to their spouse or partner
- Make sure this is legal
- Make sure they feel safe
- Know how to get rich faster
- See if this fits their comfort zone

- Find out how soon they can tell others

This makes sense. So let's take a look at the two strategies we can use to get our listeners the details they want.

DETAILS STRATEGY #1: GIVE A QUICK OVERVIEW

Every travel program will be different. There are many different travel plans, packages, cruises, holiday packages, compensation plans, and strategies.

Consider these examples only as ideas on how we can comfortably share a more expansive overview for our listeners. We will have to customize our overviews based on what we offer.

Ready for some ideas?

But first …

The company video warning

Every conversation is unique. We use our judgment to determine the best way to pass on the details to our listeners.

Here are 9 reasons to consider before "dumping off" our listener to a company video. Remember, we are not saying to never use the company video, but to consider if there is a friendlier way to get the details to our listeners.

#1. Imagine we ask a friend for details. Our friend answers, "Well, it's not worth my time to give you the details. Here is a link to a video. Figure it out yourself."

Of course, we wouldn't be this rude, but our listeners might misinterpret our intentions. People like to feel valued.

#2. Maybe we send people to a video explanation because we haven't learned anything about our business yet. This could shake the confidence our listener has in us.

#3. Some videos have links for even more details. Our listener might think, "Too many links, too complicated. This will take too long."

#4. What if our listener thinks this? "Go watch a long video? What if this video doesn't answer the questions I have? I can't risk wasting a lot of time. I'll skip watching the video."

#5. What if our listener thinks this? "I should watch the video, but I'm pressed for time. Let me look at the beginning of the video only, and see if I can find 'reasons I don't like.' Then, I can say I looked at the video, and it wasn't for me."

#6. Our listener loves scrolling through cat videos. Watching company commercials won't be fun. Our listener will choose entertainment first.

#7. Videos are one-way communication. Videos talk AT people. There is no feedback or interaction.

#8. Our listener wants to get rid of us politely. Smiles. Asks for a video link. Promises to watch the video and get back to us. Escapes from the conversation. Disappears forever.

#9. Wait! If all someone had to do was go to a website and watch videos, then why would our company even need us? Yes, our company knows that it is the personal relationship we have with listeners that makes the difference.

Okay, there are downsides to "dumping off" our listeners to watch a video.

When are company videos good?

At times, a company video is exactly what some listeners want.

These listeners are scared that we will sell and persuade them to make a bad decision.

Some listeners are time-restrained and just want to get the overview by video.

Or maybe a company video means credibility to a skeptical listener?

We do our best.

We use our judgment.

But our power is in our conversations, not in a video.

This is why our companies need us. We have the power to connect one-on-one with real people.

The short story explanation

"Here is the short story."

Wow. Magic words. Music to our listeners' ears.

Our listeners don't want long, boring PowerPoint presentations. But a short story?

That sounds great! Short is always better than long. And a story? Everyone loves stories!

The "Here is the short story" phrase has superpowers. If our listeners feel rushed for time or fear a pushy sales presentation, now they will relax.

Here are two examples of short stories to give us some creative ideas.

This first short story is for selling a travel membership. Let's imagine it is for a cruise, but we could adjust it for what we need for our program.

Short Story #1:

Us: "Do you save money every month for your annual holiday?"

Prospect: "Yes. I save $200."

Us: "Good plan. That's $2,400 available for a nice Mediterranean cruise. Plus, you will have an extra $9 in interest on your savings account. But if you use that same $200 a month in our travel club, you could get a $3,500 cruise. And I know that sounds better. You do the same thing, but you get a much better cruise.

"But oh, it gets better. If you happen to mention this travel membership with others during this upcoming year, you will get even more perks and discounts.

"So that's it. You do the same thing, but you get a lot more. Makes sense to you?"

* * *

Most listeners can do basic math. They will smile. And maybe they will have a question or two. We'll do our best to answer their questions.

This is short, friendly, and easy for our listeners to understand.

Now, what if we don't offer cruises? Well, we can adjust the story to what we offer.

But what about our business opportunity? Could we create a story that gives our listeners a great idea of what we offer that could change their lives?

Yes.

Here is a short example.

Short Story #2

Us: "Would it be okay if you never had to go to work again? So how much money would it take so that you would never have to show up for work again?"

Listener: "I could live on cheap pizza, stop commuting, watch movies, and live on the minimum of $4,000 a month as I wouldn't have many other expenses. Of course, I would like to earn more, but if I never had to work my soul-crushing job again, $4,000 would cover my expenses."

Us: "Well, you know how people love taking holidays and forgetting about their jobs for two weeks? Well, there is a company called Incredible Magic World Travel that helps people get huge discounts so they can take five-star holidays for the price of staying at a cheap hotel.

"Now, if you never wanted to go to work again, all you would have to do is help 200 families to save money by switching from their boring holidays to Incredible Magic World Travel's luxury all-inclusive holidays.

"Now, you don't know how to locate 200 families who want to switch to better holidays, but you can learn. You learned how to use a Smartphone, you learned how to get a driver's license, and you certainly can learn a system to help 200 families save money while having better holidays. And then you would earn an extra $4,000 a month.

"So what is going to be easier for you? To continue working that soul-crushing job and helping your boss get rich, or to learn a system to help 200 families save money and have holidays that they will remember forever?"

And … we're done!

Now, is this the simplified story that works for our travel business? Maybe, maybe not. But we can adjust it to our businesses. Compensation plans differ. Product offerings differ. However, we have an idea now of how we can make an effective short story that helps our listeners understand our business.

Why this works

The quick overview isn't about memorizing sales scripts, showing PowerPoint slides, or describing every part of our business.

It's about helping our listeners understand what we offer in a friendly and fast way.

Our listeners don't need every detail to decide if something feels right. They prefer a simple overview that shows the outcome. Then, if they decide they love what we offer, they can ask any question they feel is necessary.

Listeners respond to people, not pushy sales presentations.

Our value is in how we connect, listen, and explain things in a way that creates trust.

We don't have to convince anyone.

We simply give our listeners the information they want to decide for themselves.

And that's how professional networkers create a large business with calm, friendly conversations.

DETAILS STRATEGY #2: USE THESE 21 WORDS

Our listeners say, "Sounds good. Give us the details."

And then we panic. We think, "Where do I start? What should I say? Do I give a full presentation? Do I send them to a company video? Do I get them to come to a complete business presentation? What if I say too much? What if I give details that my listeners are not interested in?"

Well, good thinking. We are thinking about what our listeners really want. Good for us!

So here is how to find out exactly what our listeners want.

We ask them.

Wow. That was simple.

If we ask our listeners what details they want, it is like reading their minds. They will get the exact details they need. Nothing extra.

Bonus ... yes, there is a bonus.

When we ask our listeners what they want to know, this flips the switch in their minds. They think, "Hey, we are in control of the information. This isn't like some used car salesman giving us a monologue sales pitch. And since we are in control, we don't have to worry about some pushy or manipulative sales presentation. We like this."

We like this too. We don't have to guess. This is more relaxed for everyone.

And now, let's learn the secret.

21 words

That is the secret. All we have to do is memorize 21 words.

Oh wait! It gets easier. The reality is that we only have to learn seven words three times. We will ask three questions. Each question is only seven words. Ready?

What would you like to know first?

What would you like to know next?

What would you like to do next?

When we give answers to these three questions, our listeners love it. They don't have to sit through long videos, search complicated websites, or sit through an hour-long structured sales presentation that covers information they don't want to know.

We will give them the exact information they want ... now.

Let's go through these three questions now.

"What would you like to know first?"

Our listeners relax. They feel this is a friendly conversation. Prospects hate it when salesmen talk at them. This removes the sales tension in our listeners. This guarantees our listeners keep open minds.

Our strategy is to answer this question as fast as possible, but to be complete. An example?

Listeners: "Where is your company's home office located?"

Us: "London, England."

Done. No long, fluffy, distracting answers. We are honest and direct.

And then, we will immediately ask our second question.

"What would you like to know next?"

We continue asking the question, "What would you like to know next?"

Yes, we give short, direct answers to our listeners' most pressing questions. Then, we ask if they have more questions.

How long should we continue this?

Until our prospects run out of questions. The good news is that our listeners can only think of a few questions.

What are examples of the most common questions and our answers?

Q. "How much does it cost to join?"

A. "$99 to join. Or if you prefer, you can start at an advanced level at $349.

Q. "Have you been to the company headquarters?"

A. "Yes. I visited in December and took a tour of the offices."

Q. "When did the company start doing business?"

A. "2009."

Q. "Are the travel packages any good?"

A. "Yes. Thousands of people love our discounted travel, and they are always telling their friends about the travel deals too."

Q. "Is this a pyramid?"

A. "No."

Q. "How does the compensation plan work?"

A. "Well, if we have a lot of people decide they want to travel for less with us, we make a lot of money. If we have fewer people traveling with us, we make less.

Q. "How do the compensation plan percentages work?"

A. "You will get a chance to memorize and learn all the percentages at the training sessions."

Q. "How much money have you made so far?"

A. "Zero. Yes, I have zero profit so far. It is a business. It will take six months for me to make a good profit. Then, we will take a cruise for a week to relax. We just wanted to know if you wanted to join and work with us now, so we can cruise together. Or, if you would rather give us your address, so we can send you a postcard from our cruise."

Eventually, our listeners will run out of questions. And then we ask our third question.

"What would you like to DO next?"

Easy.

Our listeners decided to join our business a long time ago. If their original answer was "No," then we would not be this far into our conversation. All we want to know now is what they would like to do next.

Our listeners love this question. We acknowledge that they control the decisions in their lives. And we like this question too. We ask for their decision, and we allow them to make their choice. No rejection to us. It is their choice.

And what are their choices? Only two.

Choice #1. To continue their lives as they are. Keep paying more for their travel. Keep trying to get by on one paycheck.

Choice #2. To join with us now and change their future.

Remember. Closing happened long ago. They already made a decision that they want the outcome we promised.

Now we want to know what they want to do next. What is the next step for them? Here are the most common responses we could expect:

- "Okay, let's get started."
- "Sounds good. Can we pay by credit card?"
- "We would like to join. But we don't get paid until Friday. Can we join on Friday?"
- "We need to think it over." (We know this is a decision to stay where they are. And that is okay. It is their lives.)
- "Nothing good ever happens to us. We are full-time losers. We won't join as we don't want to risk the embarrassment of failure." (We grant their wish.)

And that's it.

We are done. We explained just the details our listeners wanted. We avoided a long, boring presentation.

Our listeners love it. We love it.

This isn't about giving better presentations

This is about having better conversations.

These 21 words keep everything simple. They respect our listeners' time.

We don't chase our listeners.

We don't manipulate or pressure our listeners.

We don't give flowery, long sales presentations.

Instead, we answer questions.

And then, the final decision comes naturally.

WRAPPING IT ALL UP

Do we mean closing?

Sort of, but not really.

Our listeners made their "yes" or "no" decision long ago when we started our conversation. Nobody who has made a "no" decision would ever want more details. Our listeners want what we offer.

We answered our listeners' questions. They know what we offer, the outcome, and if this fits their lives right now or not.

Now is the time for them to take action, or to postpone their action, because something personal is standing in their way.

What could stand in our listeners' way?

- Finances. Money is too tight right now.

- Fear. They are afraid of change in their lives.

- Trust. They are skeptical because we felt pushy.

- Internal programs. They don't believe they deserve something better.

Could there be more reasons? Certainly. But we get the idea.

Our listeners move forward when it feels safe for them to do so.

Now is the time for our listeners to get involved, or to keep their lives the same. That's it. Two options. Let's review.

Option #1: "Let's go!"

Option #2: "Keep our lives the same."

This is their choice. But, how do we prompt them to make a choice? How do we let our listeners know that now is the time to make up their mind without sounding pushy?

Easy.

We simply ask our listeners to pick the choice that is best for them today.

They will love this.

They get to choose. We are okay with their choices. They design their futures.

How does this sound in real life?

We ask our listeners to pick which path is easier for them. And that's it.

Examples?

"So, what is going to be easier for you? To join our travel membership now and get better holiday experiences for the same price? Or to keep taking the same ordinary, over-priced holidays every year?"

"So, what is going to be easier for you? To start your travel membership now, or to resign yourself that this summer's holiday will be at your mother-in-law's apartment with her 32 cats?"

"So, what is going to be easier for you? To continue commuting to work and suffering with your hated boss for the next 23 years? Or, to start your part-time business now, and begin building it to a full-time income as soon as possible?"

"So, what is going to be easier for you? To start saving now for that discounted cruise so that your whole family can go? Or, to continue watching other people have great holidays with their family in their social media posts?"

And now, we are silent. If our listeners are silent, it means they are thinking. Silence is okay. It is respectful. Soon, they will tell us their choice.

Not too hard. We politely give our listeners a chance to choose their futures.

And then, we are done.

When our listeners choose, what do we do next?

- We honor their choices. We move forward and help them get started.
- Or, we allow them to choose to keep their lives the same for now.

They know what we offer. If they change their minds in the future, or if their future circumstances change, they know how to contact us.

No pressure. No guilt. Just help our listeners pick their future.

Our listeners appreciate that they can design their future.

QUESTIONS AND OBJECTIONS

Questions and objections happen. But before we get too upset, let's think about this. Only the interested listeners will stay around long enough to hear the details and have questions or objections. Yes, we are only talking to the most interested people at this time.

Here's what we have accomplished so far

#1: What we offer is better than what they have now. We feel good about sharing what we offer.

#2: Relax our listener first? Yes, we took the time to connect authentically with our listeners.

#3: Introduce our offer by only talking about the outcome? We did this. Our listeners want the outcome we offer, but have some questions.

So objections are nothing more than questions that need to be answered so our listeners feel more comfortable moving ahead with our offer.

Let's take a look at the most common objections and questions.

We will answer these objections and questions as best we can. Then, our listeners will know if they are ready to move forward now or not.

Remember, we don't have to be perfect.

What we offer won't be for everyone at this exact moment in time.

We just do our best to help our listeners understand their options.

Questions and objections

Here are some common questions and objections we can expect from our curious listeners. These examples are not the only way to answer these questions, but this should give us an idea of how to answer them.

Most listeners want a simple, clear, and direct answer.

Q. I am not really clear on what you do. Explain it to me in simple sentences.

A. People pay for travel. We help them by showing them more options, great deals, and we get paid to help them.

Q. I am not sure I want to do a business. I am busy already.

A. Some people use our company only for their personal travel. Others like the idea of earning when friends travel. You can do either or both.

Q. I think your company does black magic voodoo chicken sacrifices in the jungle, and I heard you had a bad review once. And I saw a negative comment on the Internet!

A. This sounds like someone was trying to sell you or push something on you that you didn't want. I am sorry that happened. I just want to pass on to you this great option for your future travels. I hate it when people overpay for travel.

Q. I don't have time for a part-time business.

A. That is fine. You don't have to earn money when your friends travel or take holidays. You might just want to use our company only for your personal travel.

Q. I can't afford the monthly membership for this travel plan.

A. Think of the monthly membership as a savings plan for your next trip. Most people budget money every month for their personal holidays and trips. The difference is that when you save through our monthly membership, your travel savings grow even faster.

Q. Why should I join? I am already a travel agent.

A. As a travel agent, you already get some good discounts, I am sure. We can offer even more discounts and deals, so you will have more options personally. But the big reason is this. You can build a team of travel agents. You will then earn money from their travel and the travel of their clients. This can add up as your team grows.

Q. I don't travel that much. And when I think of my close friends, not many of them travel either. I am not sure this is for me.

A. Probably half of the people seldom travel or stay in budget hotels. That is okay. Our business and travel are not for them. But the other half of the people? They would love to travel more, travel better, and some even would love to have a career in travel. We help that half of the people. They are excited to learn what we have and are thrilled that we can show them great shortcuts that work.

Q. Not now. Maybe later on. Uh, I'll call you when I decide to book a trip.

A. Okay. That is the expensive way to travel, and that is okay. But if you want to save money and have better trips, start saving money now with our monthly membership. Then use these savings when you travel. Plus, if you meet someone who enjoys traveling, they could start earning you even more money before your first trip.

Q. I don't want to be a salesman. It feels icky to try to sell my friends.

A. Understand. My advice is not to be some pushy salesman with an agenda. Instead, let your friends know they can save on their travel, and even have a part-time income if they want. It is only an option. And this is up to them. No convincing. No persuading.

Most people can figure out for themselves, "Hey. Do I want to pay more for travel or less for my travel?" They will know the answer that is good for them. They don't need us to make up their minds. The math is pretty simple.

Q. I already saw something like this before.

A. Yes, people have been traveling forever, and there are lots of ways to travel. This monthly membership is a way to travel for less and get upgrades that we never thought possible. Most people would at least like to know about it.

Q. Is this a pyramid?

A. No. And it is not a lottery ticket either. We just offer great travel options to people, and we can get paid for doing this.

Q. I need to talk to my partner/spouse.

A. Good idea. Simply ask your partner/spouse these questions.

* Do you like to travel?

* Would you like to pay more for this travel or less?

That's it. Let your spouse decide for you.

Q. I want to think about this. I am not sure at this time.

A. I understand. But don't make this a big, stressful decision. I just wanted to pass on the chance where you can travel more, save big money, and have upgrades that you never imagined. That's it. And yes, you can earn money when you let others know about this also. It is always great to have extra money.

You decide if you want to save money, or to continue paying more. Up to you.

Or … how about a simpler answer to wanting to think about our offer?

A. Here are the three decisions you should make.

One: Do you plan on taking a holiday in the future?

Two: Do you want your holiday to be ordinary or an awesome experience?

Three: Do you want to keep overpaying, or finally save some money on your holidays?

Q. Is this a job?

A. No. You don't have set hours. No one will be your boss telling you when you can work or when you can't. This is a part-time business that you can plug into your life any time it feels convenient for you.

Q. How much time does this take?

A. That depends entirely on what you want to do. Some people just use the travel services and discounts. Others invest more time to create a part-time or even a full-time income.

Q. I tried network marketing before. I had a bad experience. I am not sure I want to do it again.

A. Yeah, I understand how that feels. I had a bad experience once when I ate a meal at the Taco Gastric diner. It was terrible. But I decided that I would still go out and eat at restaurants again. But of course, a different restaurant. I didn't want one bad experience control my life forever.

And what if my listeners hesitate or go quiet?

Relax. This is not a "no" decision. It just means our listeners are thinking. Give our listeners time to sort out all the things happening in their minds. Their lives are complicated. Let's respect that.

Most questions and objections are listeners telling us, "This is what is holding me back. Can you explain it a bit more so that I feel more comfortable?"

And what happens if we get really negative or sarcastic objections?

That is a clue. Our listeners feel threatened, so they make up stuff and even crazy objections. That is a sign we are being pushy with an agenda. But for most of us, this won't happen if we simply present our business as an option that can add to their lives.

SUMMARY

Let's slow everything down for a moment.

Now, we should feel less pressure, not more.

We should be more relaxed when talking with our listeners.

As an added benefit, we should feel more confident too.

When we start our network marketing travel business, it may seem a bit complicated and confusing. But if we stick to the basics, well, our business is simple.

- We don't need to convince people.

- We don't need to chase people.

- We don't need perfect presentations, perfect scripts, or perfect timing.

Instead, we focus on the big truth: "People decide fast."

Our listeners decide if they want the outcome we presented long before they want details. Once we accept this, everything gets easier.

What our business is really about

- It is not about travel websites.

- It is never about compensation plans.

- It isn't about learning clever closing techniques.

Our business is about how people actually make decisions. Once we understand how humans make decisions, everything feels simpler.

- People don't create massive pros and cons lists.
- They don't want full explanations.
- They want to know the outcome first.

And then they decide if they want what we offer or not.

If they want what we offer, then, and only then, do they want to hear the details.

If they don't want what we offer, that is okay. Life moves on.

A good way for us to look at our business is this. Our job is to offer an option.

Examples of the options we can offer?

- Better travel
- Lower costs
- More freedom
- Extra income
- Less stress

That's it. We open the door for a great outcome. We don't push people through the door. We let them choose.

We respect our listeners. We know they want control.

So we let our listeners volunteer if they want the outcome we shared with them or not.

Think of our role as this:

- Here's something that helped me.
- You decide if it fits your life.

So let's enjoy letting others know of the wonderful option we offer.

This should feel good.

We accept that some will say yes, some will say no, and some will say that now isn't a good time, but maybe later.

Their decisions are their lives.

Our obligation is to share the option of our wonderful outcome.

WHY YOU NEED TO START NETWORK MARKETING
How to Remove Risk a
Have a Better Life
KEITH SCHREITER
MAGIC WORDS FOR PROSPECTING
AUDIO
PART 1
MAGIC WORDS FOR PROSPECTING
PART 2

Learn business building skills and the mindset to make it work, check out...

BigAlBooks.com/podcast 

MORE FROM BIG AL BOOKS

See them all at BigAlBooks.com

Prospecting and Recruiting Series

10 Shortcuts Into Our Prospects' Minds
Get Network Marketing Decisions Fast!

26 Instant Marketing Ideas To Build Your Network Marketing Business

51 Ways and Places to Sponsor New Distributors
Discover Hot Prospects For Your Network Marketing Business

An Offer They Can't Refuse
14 Tools to Create Better Offers for Network Marketing

Big Al's MLM Sponsoring Magic
How To Build A Network Marketing Team Quickly

Create Influence
10 Ways to Impress and Guide Others

First Sentences for Network Marketing
How To Quickly Get Prospects On Your Side

Hooks! The Invisible Sales Superpower
Create Network Marketing Prospects Who Want to Know More

How to Get Appointments Without Rejection
Fill Our Calendars with Network Marketing Prospects

How to Get Your Prospect's Attention and Keep It!
Magic Phrases for Network Marketing

How to Meet New People Guidebook
Overcome Fear and Connect Now

How to Prospect, Sell And Build Your Network Marketing Business With Stories

Mind Reading for Network Marketing
How to Understand What Our Prospects Are Thinking

The Mini-Story Guidebook for Network Marketing
Connect and Sell in Seconds

Network Marketing One Cup at a Time
Easy connection: No rejection

Overcoming Objections
Making Network Marketing Rejection-Free

Start SuperNetworking!
5 Simple Steps to Creating Your Own Personal Networking Group

Getting Started Series

How to Build Your Network Marketing Business in 15 Minutes a Day

3 Easy Habits For Network Marketing
Automate Your MLM Success

Quick Start Guide for Network Marketing
Get Started FAST, Rejection-FREE!

Four Core Skills Series

How To Get Instant Trust, Belief, Influence and Rapport!
13 Ways To Create Open Minds By Talking To The Subconscious Mind

Ice Breakers!
How To Get Any Prospect To Beg You For A Presentation

Pre-Closing for Network Marketing
"Yes" Decisions Before The Presentation

The Two-Minute Story for Network Marketing
Create the Big-Picture Story That Sticks!

Personality Training Series (The Colors)

The Four Color Personalities for MLM
The Secret Language for Network Marketing

Mini-Scripts for the Four Color Personalities
How to Talk to our Network Marketing Prospects

Why Are My Goals Not Working?
Color Personalities for Network Marketing Success

How To Get Kids To Say Yes!
Using the Secret Four Color Languages to Get Kids to Listen

Mindset Series

Breaking the Brain Code
Easy Lessons for Your Network Marketing Career

How to Get Motivated in 60 Seconds
The Secrets to Instant Action

Secrets to Mastering Your Mindset
Take Control of Your Network Marketing Career

Presentation and Closing Series

Closing for Network Marketing
Getting Prospects Across The Finish Line

The One-Minute Presentation
Explain Your Network Marketing Business Like A Pro

How to Follow Up With Your Network Marketing Prospects
Turn Not Now Into Right Now!

Retail Sales for Network Marketers
How to Get New Customers for Your MLM Business

Leadership Series

Be the Top 1% in Network Marketing
7 Simple Steps to Leave the 99% Behind

The Complete Three-Book Network Marketing Leadership Series
Series includes: How To Build Network Marketing Leaders Volume One, How To Build Network Marketing Leaders Volume Two, and **Motivation. Action. Results.**

The Happy Network Marketer
The Wealthy & Fun Way to Build My Business

How To Build Network Marketing Leaders
Volume One: Step-By-Step Creation Of MLM Professionals

How To Build Network Marketing Leaders
Volume Two: Activities And Lessons For MLM Leaders

Motivation. Action. Results.
How Network Marketing Leaders Move Their Teams

What Smart Sponsors Do
Supercharge Our Network Marketing Team

More books...

Why You Need to Start Network Marketing
How to Remove Risk and Have a Better Life

How To Build Your Network Marketing Nutrition Business Fast

How Speakers, Trainers, and Coaches Get More Bookings
12 Ways to Flood Our Calendars with Paid Events

How To Build Your Network Marketing Utilities Business Fast

Getting "Yes" Decisions
What insurance agents and financial advisors can say to clients

Public Speaking Magic
Success and Confidence in the First 20 Seconds

Worthless Sponsor Jokes
Network Marketing Humor

ABOUT THE AUTHORS

Keith Schreiter has 30+ years of experience in network marketing and MLM. He shows network marketers how to use simple systems to build a stable and growing business.

So, do you need more prospects? Do you need your prospects to commit instead of stalling? Want to know how to engage and keep your group active? If these are the types of skills you would like to master, you will enjoy his "how-to" style.

Keith speaks and trains in the U.S., Canada, and Europe.

Tom "Big Al" Schreiter has 50+ years of experience in network marketing and MLM. As the author of the original "Big Al" training books in the late '70s, he has continued to speak in over 80 countries on using the exact words and phrases to get prospects to open up their minds and say "YES."

His passion is marketing ideas, marketing campaigns, and how to speak to the subconscious mind in simplified, practical ways. He is always looking for case studies of incredible marketing campaigns that give usable lessons.

As the author of numerous audio trainings, Tom is a favorite speaker at company conventions and regional events.

www.ingramcontent.com/pod-product-compliance
Lightning Source LLC
Chambersburg PA
CBHW071446030726
47593CB00003B/917